LET NO ONE JUDGE YOU

A PRONOMIAN POCKET GUIDE TO
COLOSSIANS 2

R.L. WATSON

Let No One Judge You: A Pronomian Pocket Guide to Colossians 2

Copyright © 2022 R. L. Watson. All rights reserved.

Pronomian Publishing LLC
Chatsworth, GA 30705

ISBN: 979-8-9851529-3-7

Publisher grants permission to reference short quotations (fewer than 300 words) in reviews, magazines, newspapers, websites, or other publications. Request for permission to reproduce more than 300 words can be made at **www.pronomianpublishing.com/contact**

Unless noted, all scriptural quotations are from The Holy Bible, English Standard Version, copyright © 2001 by Crossway Bibles, a division of Good News Publishers. Used by permission. All rights reserved.

Cover Design: Jeromy Kusch (Lanternministry.org)

LET NO ONE JUDGE YOU

A PRONOMIAN POCKET GUIDE TO COLOSSIANS 2

R. L. WATSON

CONTENTS

Editors' Preface 1

Thou Shalt Not Judge 3

Who Were the Colossian Heretics? 13

Were the Colossian Heretics Judaizers? 23

Did Jesus End the Law? 35

Conclusion 51

About the Author 55

Bibliography 57

EDITORS' PREFACE
PRONOMIAN POCKET GUIDES

Is God's Law in the Old Testament still relevant to Christians? Should Christians study and obey the Old Testament Law, or was it done away with in the New Testament? What about certain commandments from the Law, like the Sabbath, festivals, and dietary instructions? What role do these commandments have in the lives of Christians today?

When Jesus spoke about this issue, he prohibited his followers from *even thinking* that he came to abolish the Law (Matthew 5:17). Moreover, Jesus instructed his followers to do and teach *even the least* of the commandments from the Law (Matthew 5:19). Similarly, the apostle Paul affirms the Law's ongoing validity when he states that all Scripture is "profitable for teaching, for reproof, for correction, and for training in righteousness" (2 Timothy 3:16). Paul further says that one's faith does not nullify but instead establishes the Law (Romans 3:31) and that the Holy Spirit empowers Christians to keep the Law's righteous requirements (Romans 8:4). It does not seem from these passages that Jesus and Paul thought the Law was irrelevant or would become irrelevant anytime soon.

However, despite these clear biblical confirmations that the Law remains a significant part of the Christian's faith practice, other passages in the New Testament are often interpreted as saying something different. What does Paul mean when he says that Christians are no longer "under the law" (Romans 6:14), that we have "died to the law" (Romans 7:4), and that we have been "released from the law" (Romans 7:6)? What about the fact that Jesus apparently "declared all foods clean" (Mark 7:19)? What about the fact that Paul says that Christians should not judge each other regarding days and foods (Romans 14; Colossians 2)? What about the author of Hebrews' statement that there has been a "change" to the Law (Hebrews 7:12) and that the Mosaic Covenant is becoming obsolete (Hebrews 8:13)? On the surface, these passages seem to say that the Law—or at least some parts of it—have been abolished.

Is there a way to resolve this apparent contradiction? That is what the *Pronomian Pocket Guide* series seeks to do. Pronomian Publishing has partnered with several Christian teachers and scholars to tackle the question, "Is God's Law in the Old Testament still relevant to Christians?" Our authors have written detailed studies on all the important passages dealing with this question.

In this installment, R. L. Watson covers Colossians 2. Does Paul say that the Law was nailed to the cross? Does Paul imply that his readers disregarded the Law when he admonishes them not to accept judgment from people in regard to food, festivals, and the Sabbath? Watson considers these questions and more. We hope you are blessed by Watson's efforts in demonstrating that the New Testament is consistent in proclaiming the Law's ongoing validity.

David Wilber & Joshua Ensley
Pronomian Publishing LLC

CHAPTER 1
THOU SHALT NOT JUDGE

Much is made of the freedom that we have in Christ. And indeed, it should be. We are free from sin, free from death, and free from condemnation. We also come freely by his blood. And in many regards, we have degrees of freedom with how we love, serve, and worship Christ. Of course, this freedom is not license to sin (Gal. 5:13), and therefore Scripture needs to guide and inform these things, but where Scripture is silent, liberty must be extended. This is why in the beginning of Romans 14, Paul instructs his audience "not to quarrel over opinions"[1] (Rom. 14:1).

Unfortunately, there are times when people go beyond what the Bible speaks to, and there are times when people underplay what it *does* speak to. The difficulty in finding this balance comes with the general challenges of interpreting certain parts of Scripture. There are times when details of Scripture get lost in translation due to the cultural and historical separation of 2000 years, or because of the reality that there are things that are difficult to understand (2 Pet. 3:16). Sometimes, confusion comes because passages are read through the tradition handed down to us, and we assume that the Bible says things that it doesn't. These are claims like, "Jesus was born on the 25th of December," that "money is the root of all evil," and that "God won't give you more than you can handle." Another popular pseudo-passage of Scripture is the claim, "Jesus said it is un-Christian to judge." For some, this allusion to Matthew 7:1 ("Judge not, that you be not judged") is taken to mean that it is wrong to tell someone that something controversial

---

1   *Dialogismos*: the thinking of a man deliberating with himself (cf. Col 2:8, 22).

is sinful, or in some extremes, to tell someone that something they said is theologically incorrect. As Eric Bargerhuff writes:

> One could easily argue that Matthew 7:1 is by far the most frequently misapplied verse in the entire Bible, used and abused by both Christians and non-Christians alike. Those who mishandle this verse often use it as a "shield for sin," a barrier to keep others at bay, allowing them to justify living as they please without regard for moral boundaries or accountability.[2]

Additionally, sometimes this verse is used to accompany the advice that Christians need to be "more loving." This is based on a belief in the supposed eleventh commandment, *thou shalt be nice*, where "being loving" means to never hurt someone's feelings. However, as we read on in Matthew 7, we find that Christians are to judge[3] between the narrow and wide gate (Matt. 7:13-14), the false prophet from the true (Matt. 7:15-20), and identify the "dog" and the "pig" (Matt. 7:6). And earlier in the Sermon on the Mount, Jesus had been teaching the difference between sin and righteousness so that we may judge rightly. What is forbidden in Matthew 7:1 is the more negative connotations of *krino* (judging). Specifically, Jesus denounces unfairly and severely rejecting or condemning someone by calling out their sins without any concern for personal repentance (Matt. 7:3-5). Hence, we can see that Jesus is *not* opposed to moral judgements and accountability. Instead, he is opposed to prideful and hypocritical judgement.

---

2 Eric J. Bargerhuff, *The Most Misused Verses in the Bible: Surprising Ways God's Word Is Misunderstood* (Grand Rapids, MI: Baker Publishing Group, 2012), 25.
3 *Krino*: distinguish, discern right from wrong.

This is why we must take the time to stop and look at what passages of Scripture actually say. We can do this by taking the time to exegete passages, follow the flow of arguments, understand the meanings of words as the original audience would have understood them, as well as take into consideration the whole counsel of God. We do, indeed, need to test our doctrine often and break through our lens of tradition and preferences with Scripture.

Another passage that tends to get misunderstood and misused with regards to passing judgement is found in Colossians 2. It is a passage that is cited to support the claim that there are certain expressions of the Christian faith that are non-binding on us, and therefore one should not be negatively condemned or even disqualified for not doing them. Indeed, there are certainly disciplines and practices where we have liberty and freedom of conscience when it comes to things such as speaking in tongues, tithing,[4] fasting, or alcohol. Or perhaps, in more extreme circles, it concerns judging others based on the use and "correct pronunciation" of the "sacred names" of Yeshua and YHWH, or reading the "correct" translation of Scripture. In all these matters, one cannot say that another follower of Christ is not a real Christian because they do, or do not do, these things. Our identity in Christ is not founded on such things, and Scripture is either silent on these matters or non-dogmatic in their expression. For instance, Scripture says Christians need to gather regularly, and describes the purpose and general content of those gatherings, but is silent regarding the form and shape. Thus, liberty is given, and should be given, in these areas.

So, when these key verses in Colossians 2 are quoted, they are typically used to argue that these practices are not only non-binding,

---

[4] More specifically, giving a literal "ten percent," rather than giving in general. Those who belong to Christ should be generous.

but also in a variety of degrees, abolished. My focus in this book is to address the role of Colossians 2 in this debate concerning the continuity of the Law of God into the New Testament, and by extension, the New Covenant. This is a huge topic with a wide variety of perspectives and many "moving parts,"[5] but for the purposes of this short book, we will focus on this chapter of Scripture.

The Colossian Arguments

Two key passages referenced in Colossians 2 are used by those who take the position that the Law is not for Christians. One is found when Paul describes the new life we have in Christ because of the crucifixion:

> And you, who were dead in your trespasses and the uncircumcision of your flesh, God made alive together with him, having forgiven us all our trespasses, by *canceling the record of debt that stood against us with its legal demands. This he set aside, nailing it to the cross.*
> —Colossians 2:13-14 (emphasis added)

According to those who argue for the end of the Law, this passage teaches that the Law was nailed to the cross, thus putting an end to its relevance. As *GotQuestions.com* claims, "None of the Old Testament law is binding on Christians today. When Jesus died on the cross, he put an end to the Old Testament law."[6] According to one Pastor, the

---

5 I have covered this topic in much more detail in *Why then the Law* (2020) and *Forgotten Covenant* (2021).

6 "Do Christians have to obey the Old Testament law?," *Got Questions Ministries*, January 4, 2022, https://www.gotquestions.org/Christian-law.html.

"ordinances that were against us" is "referring to the Law of God."[7] He goes on to explain:

> ...when Jesus died on the cross he took care of the law and it says there that it was against us. How graphically he describes it there, handwriting of ordinance that was against us, so he blotted it out. It was like having a debt, and the blotter and just wipe out the debt. It was against us, it was contrary to us and then the second thing he did he took it out of the way by nailing it to his cross.[8]

Likewise, another Pastor explains how verse 14 teaches that

> ...[God] canceled the debt, and what is the debt? I think it's two things. One, I think it's our sin, but also when you look at the passage... "it's legal demands," what's that? You know the first five books of the Old Testament, it's called the law. You know what the purpose of the law is? To show us that we're sinners. That's the whole purpose of it. I'm not called to live to the standard of the law... the purpose of law is to show 'hey I'm a sinner I can't save myself.' So, God erased it, blotted it out, moved us from an Old Covenant to a New Covenant.[9]

This interpretation is similar to what Michael Bird says in his commentary on Colossians:

---

[7] John Miller, "Complete In Christ - Part 2," *Revival Christian Fellowship*, July 2, 2017, https://www.revival.tv/sermons/colossians/complete-in-christ-part-2/.
[8] Ibid.
[9] Brian Holland, "The Book of Colossians: Colossians 2:9-15," *Ignite City Church*, June 26, 2022, https://youtu.be/pXALiCDARQ8.

> The Torah became an instrument of death only through sin and it was designed to be in effect only until the coming of the Messiah...The angelic powers that seek to use the Torah to subjugate the believers find the weapon snatched from their grasp and nailed to the cross.[10]

There is, however, some variation in the interpretation of verse 14. In his article on the passage, Edwin Reynolds nuances the act of nailing the Law to the cross:

> Christ effectually nailed *the ritual law* to the cross, so putting an end to the distinctions between Jews and Gentiles and paving the way for the spread of the gospel to all the world through faith in Christ as opposed to coming to God through the sanctuary and its rituals.[11]

Thus, we encounter two schools of thought when it comes to the Law. One is that the Law is done away with completely (the abolitionist), and the other is that the Law has ongoing relevance except for the ceremonial aspects. This book will attempt to address both.

And so, having read this passage in this light, when those who argue for the end of the Law move into the next section, they read the main passage that this book will consider through this lens of abolishment, which is verses 16-17:

---

10 Michael Bird, *Colossians and Philemon: A New Covenant Commentary* (United Kingdom: Lutterworth Press, 2011), 81.

11 Edwin Reynolds, "'Let No One Judge You': Col 2:16-17 in Exegetical Perspective," *Journal of the Adventist Theological Society*, 20/1-2 (2009), 220.

> Therefore let no one pass judgment on you in questions of food and drink, or with regard to a festival or a new moon or a Sabbath. These are a shadow of the things to come, but the substance belongs to Christ.
> —Colossians 2:16-17

The interpretation that is often made is that since, according to verse 14, the Law is no longer relevant or binding on the Christian, one cannot judge them for not observing things like food laws, festivals, or Sabbaths. Therefore, these practices have no ongoing validity or relevance for the follower of Christ. This argument can be divided into two parts.

The first argument concerns verse 16 and the nature of the "Colossian heresy." The claim goes that based on the use of "distinctive Jewish identity markers,"[12] the Colossian believers were being pressured to participate in these ceremonial aspects of the Law in order to be true and complete Christians. As David Garland explains, the false teaching "passes judgement on the Colossians for not submitting to the observances of certain holy days and food and purity restrictions (2:16). [And failing to do so] will disqualify them in some way or rob them of the prize" of the fullness of God in Christ.[13] F. F. Bruce makes a similar argument. Drawing from the Galatians situation, he says:

> As the Galatians' observance of 'days and months and seasons and years' was a sign of their renewed and untimely subjection to the 'weak and beggarly elemental forces' (Gal 4:9-10), the same could be said of the Christians in Colossae or elsewhere

---

12 David Garland, *Colossians, Philemon* (Grand Rapids, MI: Zondervan, 2009), 30.
13 Ibid., 25.

if they allowed themselves to be dictated to with regards to the observance of [Jewish festivals].[14]

Thus, Christians observing the "Jewish" festivals and food laws, would be an unnecessary and detrimental return to a "weak and beggarly" yoke. To verify the unnecessary nature of these practices, it is suggested that their purposes make them no longer necessary. According to Gregory Beale, the first and primary purpose "of these [ceremonial] laws in the OT was to enable the Israelite to become clean and be able to enter into God's temple to worship him."[15] Bird likewise argues that "Adherence to the food laws was a matter of purity and election since they kept the Israelites separate from the other nations and preserved their capacity to worship God in a state of ritual purity."[16] Therefore, for Gentiles—who most likely made up a majority of the church in Colossae—those practices are irrelevant since they were intended to keep the Gentile out. This is why F. F. Bruce argues that "The observance of the sacred calendar, like the observance of the Levitical food laws, was obligatory on Jews. But Christians are free from obligations of this kind."[17]

The second part of the argument relates to the other claimed purpose of the ceremonial laws, namely their revelational function. This is drawn from verse 17, which says that these practices were "shadows of the things to come." Thus, the argument goes that since the substance (i.e., Christ) has come, the shadows are no longer relevant. Or

---

14   F. F. Bruce, *The Epistles to the Colossians, to Philemon, and to the Ephesians* (United Kingdom: Eerdmans Publishing Company, 1984), 19.
15   G. K. Beale, *Colossians and Philemon* (Grand Rapids, MI: Baker Publishing Group, 2019), 13.
16   Bird, 84.
17   Bruce, 114.

as F. F. Bruce phrases it, "it is as members of the body of Christ that his people now possess the substance, so that they may cheerfully let the shadow go."[18] Likewise, Bird, alluding to Romans 10, states "For Paul, the goal of the Torah has reached its completion in Jesus, so that to turn to the Torah for the basis of their identity, way of life, or salvation is to return to an obsolete and even oppressive situation."[19] As mentioned above, a more nuanced interpretation of the relevance of the Law would argue with Reynolds that "The ritual law consisted of types and ceremonies which foreshadowed the atoning work of Christ and had no more function after Christ came as the real Sacrifice, the Body to which the shadow points."[20]

Summary

Having considered the arguments of a number of commentators and pastors, we can summarize their interpretation of the claims of Colossians 2 regarding the Law as follows:

The false teachers in Colossae were wrong in forcing the Colossian Christians to accept Jewish rituals because:

- The Law, either just the ceremonial aspects or the whole, has no binding authority over the Christian since Jesus nailed it to the cross.
- The coming of Christ fulfilled their purposes of foreshadowing his ministry and purifying the worshiper so they can approach God.
- The ending of Jew and Gentile division in the Gospel means that their dividing purpose is unnecessary.

---

18 Ibid., 117.
19 Bird., 73-74.
20 Reynolds, 211.

Therefore, the observance of food laws, festivals, and sabbaths becomes a matter of "opinion" (cf. Rom. 14:1), and the Christian who does not observe cannot be judged by those who do.

But is this correct? Does this passage of Scripture teach that the Law as a whole, if not the ceremonial law, was abolished with the coming of Christ? In the following chapters of this book, I will seek to answer this question. I will consider each of these claims by looking at these verses in their wider context as well as testing the rationale for the arguments mentioned above.

CHAPTER 2
WHO WERE THE COLOSSIAN HERETICS?

One of the most interesting parts of my study tour to Turkey was the visit to Colossae. Having come from Ephesus where significant reconstruction had taken place, I arrived at a large mound of dirt with some marble fragments on top and told, "This is Colossae." In a similar manner, the details behind the letter to the Colossians are also a hidden mystery. Without Paul naming the group, nor addressing detailed claims made by them, much of the Colossian heresy can only be put together with inference using the little clues we have. On the one hand, this helpfully makes the application more universal as the letter's content can be used "to oppose any false form of religion that involves knowledge or works with true religion, namely, a personal relationship with Jesus Christ…"[1] On the other hand, it adds a layer of difficulty when interpreting what exactly it is that Paul is warning his audience against, leaving the modern reader to make inferences to fill in the silences. Although many are reasonable, it does become possible to make claims that the letter does not. So, in order to test the claims made in the introduction, we need to see what we can know about the Colossian heresy to know what Paul was rebuking and telling the Colossians to reject.

Most commentators acknowledge a number of possibilities, and many put forward similar theories. Due to the scope of this book, it is not possible to include a detailed analysis and evaluation of each

---

1 Edwin Reynolds, "'Let No One Judge You': Col 2:16-17 in Exegetical Perspective," *Journal of the Adventist Theological Society*, 20/1-2 (2009), 209-210.

model, especially in light of the fact that a lack of evidence makes it difficult to know for certain. We will, however, consider the general nature and content of the Colossian heretics' teaching that Paul does include in this letter.

The Nature of the Colossian Philosophy

We get a good description of the Colossian heresy in verse 8 when Paul says, "See to it that no one takes you captive by philosophy and empty deceit, according to human tradition, according to the elemental spirits of the world, and not according to Christ." This verse reveals three key descriptions.

First, it is a philosophy based on human tradition. It is important to note that in the ancient world, the word philosophy had a much broader meaning and application than it does today. It was a term used to describe a wide range of belief systems, including religious ones. By warning that this philosophy is shaped by human tradition, Paul is most likely saying that the source of the philosophy's content is informed by human speculation rather than divine revelation—in particular, revelation through Christ.[2] This is why Paul later says that the Colossian philosophy has "the *appearance* of wisdom" (Col. 2:23, emphasis added), for earlier in the chapter he had told the Colossians that it is *in Christ* that "all the treasures of wisdom and knowledge" are hidden (Col. 2:3). Some commenters, such as Bird, recognize the similarity of Jesus' critique in Mark 7:9, and suggest the term "tradition" (*paradodis*) is a "Christian jibe at certain Jewish exspansive inter-

---

2 Douglass Moo, *The Letters to the Colossians and to Philemon* (United Kingdom: Eerdmans Publishing Company, 2008), 187.

pretations of the Torah,"[3] arguing that the Colossian philosophy is quite Jewish in nature. However, although the argument and criticism are similar, "the language is too general to justify such an inference,"[4] and therefore all that is clear is that he is making the same point that their traditions are not founded on divine truth. This is not to say that traditions are inherently bad, but they can become problematic when they replace Scripture in forming the foundation of why they are done.

Second, the content of the Colossian philosophy is "empty deceit." If this philosophy was a breakfast cereal, then its teachings about having a relationship with God have the spiritual sustenance value of the cardboard box. Or to use another dietary analogy, they are "empty carbs"—foods high in sugar that have little to no nutritional value. That this teaching is "empty" means it is "devoid of intellectual, moral, or spiritual value."[5] That it is "deceptive" means it leads to what is false and destructive—false because, as mentioned above, it is not based in Christ, and destructive because it consequently leads its follower away from Christ. This description, according to Ben Witherington, is a warning of the "grave danger of Christians who are prone to listen to such powerful persuasion and to be influenced by it."[6] Such a danger is evident in the use of the phrase, "take you captive" (*sylagogon*), which in the Greek "is regularly used of taking captives in war and leading them away as booty, [thus depicting] the

---

[3] Michael Bird, *Colossians and Philemon: A New Covenant Commentary* (United Kingdom: Lutterworth Press, 2011), 75.
[4] Moo, 50 (cf. 187).
[5] Ibid., 186.
[6] Ben Witherington, *The Letters to Philemon, the Colossians, and the Ephesians: A Socio-Rhetorical Commentary on the Captivity Epistles* (United Kingdom: Eerdmans Publishing Company, 2007), 154.

false teachers as 'man stealers' wishing to entrap the Colossians and drag them away into spiritual enslavement."[7]

This brings us to the third detail, namely that the teaching is dependent on, and focused on, the "elemental spirits" and forces of this world. One of the issues with the word describing this content (*stoicheia*) is that it is a broad term in the ancient world, but it can be summarized into three key uses. One is that this term refers to the foundational universal elements like water, fire, and earth; another is that it refers to the essential, foundational principles of an area of study, such as learning the letters before one can read; and thirdly, it is a reference to spiritual beings. The issue, as many commentators identify, is that each option has contextual and lexical weight to it. The two strongest, according to Douglass Moo, are the third[8] and the first.[9] Moo reasons that there is actually not much reason to divide these two based on the Ancient World's cosmology:

> The Colossian 'philosophy,' by its preoccupation with rules about material things, was, in Paul's view, treating them like the pagans did, as if they were fundamental cosmic powers that needed to be placated. They were, in effect, putting them in the place of Christ... and failing to recognize that believers had 'died' to them in Christ (v. 20).[10]

---

[7] Curtis Vaughan, "Colossians," *The Expositors Bible Commentary - Vol 11* (Grand Rapids, MI: Zondervan, 1978), 197-198.

[8] Contextually strong—cf. Col 2:15,18; 1:16; Gal 4:3,8-9. Consider too that the focus and content of the philosophy is juxtaposed with Christ, a personal being.

[9] Lexically strong—it was the most common meaning in usage in Paul's day.

[10] Moo, 191.

Hence, here is the danger Paul warned about: the philosophy threatens to lead his audience away under the influence of demonic forces (1 Cor. 10:20) as it encourages its adherents to inadvertently worship them through various rituals and practices as they seek spiritual fulfilment and enlightenment. As Moo describes, "The false teachers were appealing to spiritual beings, visions, and rules to find security in this very uncertain universe. In doing so, they were questioning the sufficiency of Christ."[11]

Thus far, we can determine that the Colossian heresy, or philosophy, had the following characteristics: it was false and dangerous, it was based on human speculation rather than divine revelation, and it inadvertently led to the worship of demons, which suggests it was demonically inspired as well.

The Content of the Colossian Philosophy

Paul gives us more clues about what "living the philosophy" looks like. At the end of this chapter, Paul warns the Colossians with the following imperative:

> Let no one disqualify you, insisting on asceticism and worship of angels, going on in detail about visions, puffed up without reason by his sensuous mind...If with Christ you died to the elemental spirits of the world, why, as if you were still alive in the world, do you submit to regulations — "Do not handle, Do not taste, Do not touch" (referring to things that all perish as they are used) — according to human precepts and teachings? These have indeed an appearance of wisdom in promoting self-made religion and asceticism and severity to

---

11   Ibid., 60.

> the body, but they are of no value in stopping the indulgence of the flesh.
> —Colossians 2:18, 20-23

A significant aspect of the philosophy involved the practice of aestheticism. The original Greek makes use of the term "humility" (*tapeinophrosyne*), however, this is a term often associated with practices such as fasting (Psa. 35:13; Isa. 58:30) and would reflect the passage's description of the restrictions placed on food and drink (Col. 2:16, 21-22). It also reflects the words of verse 23 that describe the intention of "stopping the indulgences of the flesh." Vaughan in his commentary explains, "For ascetics, the body is a thing to be buffeted and punished... They see the body as evil and conclude that the way to holiness is to deny all the body's desires."[12] This, along with other ascetic and ritual observances, is described in general as "harsh treatment of the body," rather than self-flagellation or mutilation. The irony of the mention of humility[13] is that their asceticism (along with their other practices) made them "puffed-up" and arrogant towards those who were not "as devoted as they were." It is suggested that there is a connection to the Mosaic law in these prohibitions, however, the rules described in verse 21 ("Do not handle, Do not taste, Do not touch") in combination with the nature of the philosophy explained above and its elements described below, suggest that they "were doubtless prohibitions stemming from pagan asceticism."[14]

---

12 Vaughan, 206.
13 Quite likely a term used by the Colossian heretics, as are "wisdom," "self-imposed religion," and "severe treatment of the body." See Clinton Arnold, *The Colossian Syncretism: The Interface Between Christianity and Folk Belief at Colossae* (Germany: J.C.B. Mohr, 1995), 200.
14 Vaughan, 207.

The next feature of the philosophy concerns the worship of angels. The translation of this phrase (*threskeia ton angelon*) can either be worship with angels, or worship of angels. Although, as Douglas Moo identifies, "Such a participation with angels in the worship of God in heaven features in many Jewish mystical and apocalyptic writings,"[15] he does go on to say that the more common usage of the phrase (historically) refers to the worship offered *to* angels, which corresponds to the letter's focus of Jesus' superiority over spiritual beings. Moreover, as Clinton Arnold identifies, there is evidence that in both the ancient world, and within the region of Colossae, the invocation and veneration of angels for protection, deliverance, and connection with higher deities was common among pagan angel-cults, as well as syncretistic Christians and Jewish mystics who practiced magic.[16] This relates to the idea of "having the appearance of wisdom." In the context of magical practices, "wisdom" is the way of describing an "expertise in manipulating the spirit world and bringing the hostile 'powers' under control."[17] Thus, the teachers of the philosophy[18] believed they could manipulate spiritual powers for their benefit, but as Paul critiques, it is simply an "appearance," for it is "empty deceit" and "human tradition" (Col. 2:8).

The third feature helps us to understand some of the purpose of fasting. It was believed that by fasting, one was preparing himself for visionary experiences, which was considered a significant part of mystery cult initiation, where one can find enlightenment and empowerment, as well as be able to encounter gods and goddesses. Thus,

---

15 Moo, 226-227.
16 Arnold, 59, 88-89.
17 Ibid., 202. Cf. Wis 7:17-20.
18 See Ibid., 205: "esoteric knowledge expressed through magical practices was also termed 'philosophy.'"

because the teacher is initiated and the Colossian Christians are not, the Colossian Christians are being condemned and pressured to do the same.[19] Arnold explains that this likewise links to the idea of honor (v. 23)[20] that the false teachers "believe God confers upon them through visionary appearance, his election, bestowal of divine power, and possibly mystical union with him."[21] Thus, visions, indeed all practices of the philosophy,[22] are a point of pride and an "indulgence of the flesh" (Gal. 5:19-21).

The final element of the philosophy is that it is freely chosen. Paul uses the term "self-imposed worship," describing the voluntary nature of membership in the mystery cults. As opposed to other religions in the ancient world, they were not prescribed or defined by one's family, status, or region; people decide to become devotees of various divine beings and participate in their rituals as they draw nearer to them for their own blessings. This, Burkert explains, suggests a sense of "personal closeness to some great divinity."[23] Such a claim would no doubt be a point of pride ("I am wise enough to choose this enlightened path"), and a way to obtain favor from the gods and goddesses ("Bless me, for I chose to follow you").

Summary

Having considered the nature and the content of the Colossian philosophy, we can observe that there was a significant mystical element to it. It appears that these teachers were telling the Colossian

---

19 Ibid., 122-123.
20 *Timē*: translated "value."
21 Arnold, 219.
22 As evidenced by the relative pronoun *hostis* at the beginning of the list in verse 23.
23 Walter Burkert, *Ancient Mystery Cults* (United Kingdom: Harvard University Press, 1987), 11.

Christians that if they want to have the fullness of God and the fullness of his blessings, they needed to engage in their aesthetic practices, worship and invoke angels to ward off evil spirits, and seek visionary experiences. Such a message would certainly be appealing to a society in a region where folk religions were shaped by what Plutarch called "demon terror" (*Moralia* 164-171), which resulted in the widespread use of spells, magic, and bodily abuse. For Christians to adopt the Colossian Philosophy, as Paul identifies, is a great error. Not only is it all based on human speculation and traditions, but it is also a denial of the true supremacy of Christ. As Douglas Moo explains, "The false teachers were appealing to spiritual beings, visions, and rules to find security in this very uncertain universe. In doing so, they were questioning the sufficiency of Christ."[24] Considering the amount of space devoted to this theme in the letter, the exaltation and supremacy of Jesus is clearly Paul's main concern and counter-argument to the Colossian Philosophy.

This leaves one final passage that describes the teachings of the philosophy, namely the one mentioning "food and drink, festivals, new moons and Sabbaths." Does this verse indicate that the Colossian heretics were Judaizers? And consequently, does Paul's rebuttal teach that the ceremonial aspects of the Law, namely the food laws, festivals, and Sabbaths, are abolished? These two questions will be the focus of the following chapters.

---

24 Moo, 60.

CHAPTER 3
WERE THE COLOSSIAN HERETICS JUDAIZERS?

A major theme in the book of Hebrews is the superiority of the ministry of Christ over and against that of Moses, in particular, with regards to the Aaronic Priesthood. In the book, the author seeks to explain how Jesus is able to achieve not only more effectively, but more extensively, that which was foreshadowed in the practices of the priesthood. The High Priest lived and died; Jesus makes intercession forever. Sacrifices were presented daily, not only for the High Priest, but also daily for the people; Jesus' sacrifice was once for all. Those sacrifices could only purify the flesh; the atonement of the Messiah cleansed the conscience. The list goes on. And this is the aim of the author of Hebrews: "to point out the supremacy of Christ over everything to which the readers might be tempted to turn...Therefore, the readers must hold fast to Jesus Christ."[1]

This is a very similar core theme and message as in the letter to the Colossian church. In the opening one and a half chapters, Paul has highlighted the superiority and supremacy of Christ over all things before turning to critique the empty tradition that may lead them astray. His point is that everything promised by the Colossian heretics is not only false and empty, but finds true and even greater fulfilment in Christ.

---

1   Richard D. Phillips, *Hebrews* (New Jersey: P & R Publishing, 2006), 8.

Verse 16

In the middle of his rebuttal to the false teachers, Paul gives the following instruction: "Therefore let no one pass judgment on you in questions of food and drink, or with regard to a festival or a new moon or a Sabbath" (Col. 2:16). As I noted in chapter 1, it is suggested that this is evidence of the Christians at Colossae being pressured to turn to the Torah and practice the ceremonial aspects of the Law, namely food laws, festivals, and sabbaths. And indeed, there is definitely a Jewish influence here. The collection of terms as a phrase does appear in a number of Old Testament passages. For example, "And I will put an end to all her mirth, her feasts, her new moons, her Sabbaths, and all her appointed feasts" (Hos. 2:11); "It shall be the prince's duty to furnish the burnt offerings, grain offerings, and drink offerings, at the feasts, the new moons, and the Sabbaths..." (Eze. 45:17); and "The contribution of the king from his own possessions was for the burnt offerings: the burnt offerings of morning and evening, and the burnt offerings for the Sabbaths, the new moons, and the appointed feasts..." (2 Chr. 31:3). Thus, there appears to be a clear influence of those ritual and ceremonial aspects mentioned in the Law on the Colossian Philosophy.

Consequently, based on the letter's similar message to Hebrews and the nature of this warning in 2:16, it is concluded—as mentioned in the opening chapter—that Paul's message is, "Do not let people tell you that you need to follow the ceremonial law." The question of how the front of the Bible relates to the back belongs to a bigger issue in which there are a range of positions. One claim is that the only commandments that are applicable for believers are the ones in the New Testament. Thus, for those who hold such a position, this and verse 14 (addressed later) are warnings against following the Law.

At face value, it does appear that Paul is putting these practices into the "opinion"[2] folder and that his critique of the false teachers is similar to that of the Judaizers in Galatia (e.g., Gal. 1:6-9). However, there are a number of contextual issues with the interpretation that this philosophy was a type of Judaizing and that Paul is addressing a situation similar to what he addressed in Galatia.

The first issue is the tone of Paul's letter. The argumentation against the philosophy and its teachers in Colossae is much more restrained than those in Galatia. Consider how, in Galatians, Paul sarcastically hopes those of the circumcision party "emasculate themselves" (Gal. 5:12) and calls them "accursed" (Gal. 1:8-9). He also calls those who are falling for the circumcision party's doctrine "foolish," and uses sarcasm to ask quite sternly why they are deserting the Gospel and who has "bewitched" them (Gal. 1:6-7). Also, note the absence of thanksgiving and encouragement regarding their faith in the opening chapter, suggesting both a high level of tension and urgency regarding the theological conflict in Galatia. This level of force and urgency are missing in his letter to Colossae. Although Paul uses strong language to describe the false nature of the philosophy, as well as highlighting the arrogance of the false teachers, he spends far more time making a positive case for true doctrine than critiquing and condemning false doctrine. Moreover, he spends a notable space of his introduction in the letter making thanksgiving for his readers' faith and encourages them to persevere, speaking positively of their security in Christ. The tone is clearly different, thus revealing a much less urgent and anxious situation. Indeed, Paul reacted strongly to Judaizers (Acts 15:2) as well as to the idea of justification by works, and works of the law. This notable difference in Paul's reaction makes it unlikely that he was addressing Judaizers in

---

2   See Chapter 1.

Colossae. It could be argued that the urgency in Galatians is due to the fact that they had accepted the teaching, but it appears that this had happened in Colossae too (Col. 2:20). On its own, this is not enough to rule it out completely, but there are other omissions and features that suggest Judaizing was not the issue at Colossae.

The second issue is that there is a significant topic missing from not only this chapter but also the book of Colossians as a whole. And that is circumcision. Unlike in Galatians (Gal. 5:2-11; 6:12-13), at no point in the letter does Paul warn against circumcision, nor does he mention that the false teachers were promoting the practice. Sabbaths, food restrictions, and festivals were all significant Jewish identity markers in the first century, but circumcision was much more so. This is why those mentioned in Acts 15 insisted on Gentiles being circumcised. They believed it necessary to be circumcised in order to be brought into Israel so they can be saved.[3] And yet, despite the centrality of circumcision to the theology of the Judaizers, Colossians is silent on circumcision with regards to the philosophy. As Ben Witherington explains:

> [U]nlike in Galatians, Paul makes no direct reference to the false philosophy requiring circumcision. The circumcision language is used here only in the double metaphor of the physical death of Jesus and the spiritual death of the old nature of the convert. This internal transformation of the

---

3   There are many occurrences of the Greek word for Judaize (become a Jew) that include the act of circumcision in ancient writings, e.g., Est. 8:15; Josephus, *Wars of the Jews* 2.454.

convert in part entails the receiving of forgiveness for all wrongdoing.[4]

Were the false teachers Judaizers, Paul would certainly have addressed the theology of circumcision in a practical and scriptural matter, and not merely in a figurative way. Thus, the reader cannot draw too much of a similarity between the situation in Galatia and Colossae. So, what then are we to make of the reference to these Jewish practices? Why would these false teachers be pushing their followers to practice these, but not circumcision?

The Philosophers' Food and Festivals

As mentioned previously, we need to consider the other descriptive details of the Colossian Philosophy in order to understand the relevance of Paul's mention of food, festivals, and Sabbaths. Is it possible that instead of being members of the Circumcision Party or Judaizers, Paul was rebuking and warning against possible Christians[5] who were insisting that the church must follow these ceremonial aspects of the Law, if not the Law as a whole? If, as it is claimed, that obedience to the Law is part of the Colossian philosophy, then the descriptions Paul gives to these teachings would need to be applied to the Law. However, when we consider the descriptions analyzed in the previous chapter, it becomes quite unlikely. For if these descriptions *were* applied to the Law as well, it would be rather problematic.

---

4   Ben Witherington, *The Letters to Philemon, the Colossians, and the Ephesians: A Socio-Rhetorical Commentary on the Captivity Epistles* (United Kingdom: Eerdmans Publishing Company, 2007), 158.

5   It is considered that the reference to not "holding fast to the Head [Christ]" (2:19) means the false teaching is coming from within. See Douglass Moo, *The Letters to the Colossians and to Philemon* (United Kingdom: Eerdmans Publishing Company, 2008), 51.

There are numerous places in his letters where Paul speaks of the Law positively. For example, "Do we then overthrow the law by this faith? By no means! On the contrary, we uphold the law" (Rom 3:31); "So the law is holy, and the commandment is holy and righteous and good" (Rom 7:12); "All Scripture is breathed out by God and profitable for teaching, for reproof, for correction, and for training in righteousness, that the man of God may be complete, equipped for every good work" (2 Tim. 3:16); and "'Honor your father and mother' (this is the first commandment with a promise)" (Eph. 6:2), to quote a few. Were Paul to begin to deride the Law of God, he would be in contradiction not only with himself, but also with the Holy Spirit who spoke through David (Acts 1:16; 4:25):

> The law of the Lord is perfect, reviving the soul…the precepts of the Lord are right, rejoicing the heart…the rules of the Lord are true, and righteous altogether. More to be desired are they than gold, even much fine gold; sweeter also than honey and drippings of the honeycomb.
> —Psalm 19:7-10

> Oh how I love your law! It is my meditation all the day. Your commandment makes me wiser than my enemies, for it is ever with me. I have more understanding than all my teachers, for your testimonies are my meditation…How sweet are your words to my taste, sweeter than honey to my mouth!
> —Psalm 119:97, 103

In light of these positive descriptions, not only in the Psalms but also in the letters of Paul, how can we say that the negative descriptions given to the Colossian philosophy are consistent with how the Bible describes God's law? For if the need to observe the ceremonial law were a part of the Colossian Philosophy that Paul was warning against, then his attitudes towards and descriptions of what the false teachers were teaching would need to be applied to not just the ceremonial law but the Law as a whole. Some like to divide the Law into moral, civil, and ceremonial categories, and distinguish between them. However, the ceremonial aspects are still a part of the Divine Law and part of the divine revelation of Yahweh's righteousness. So, can we apply the following descriptions to the divine revelation of God's righteousness and holiness?

- Empty deceit
- Human tradition
- Submission to elemental (demonic) spirits
- In opposition to Christ
- Human precepts and teaching
- Having the appearance of wisdom
- Self-made religion
- Promoting severe[6] punishment to the body

Surely not. These descriptions are far from the positive and beneficial descriptions Paul provides in 2 Timothy. Granted, it can be agreed that the Law is "of no value in stopping the indulgence of the flesh," but that does not account for the other descriptions. Thus, the false teacher's insistence on the ceremonial practices included in the Law needs to be understood from a perspective that is beyond a mere promotion of Torah observance. As Clinton Arnold explains, "The sum total of this terminology seems to go beyond the cultic and ritual

---

6   *Apheidia*: unsparing severity.

practices typical of Judaism."[7] Understanding the religious world of the region of Colossae will help make sense of Paul's prohibition.

As mentioned earlier, folk religion and mystery cults were commonplace in the Phrygian area. These people were quite superstitious when it came to "omens," seeing every tragedy (big or small) as an attack from demonic forces or divine disfavor, and thus the religions had a focus on using charms, spells, and intermediaries—human or angelic—to find deliverance. They were also henotheistic,[8] showing they were quite prone to syncretism, renaming deities or adding them to their pantheon. For example, due to the Hellenization of the region, the local fertility "mother goddess" of the region was renamed after a Greek goddess, becoming "Artemis of Ephesus." It is against this background that Clinton Arnold concludes that the Colossian philosophy was "a combination of Phrygian folk belief, local folk Judaism [which itself was already syncretized with local mysticism and magic], and Christianity."[9] Indeed, such a combination better reflects the negative description of the false teachings we have considered in the book thus far compared to mere Torah observance. Moreover, it accounts for why Paul would be concerned that the Colossian Christians would find the teaching appealing—syncretism and demon terror is part of their previous worldview. The statement, "with Christ you died to the elemental spirits of the world" (Col. 2:20) shows that his audience has previous experience engaging with the mystery cult practices, and his repeated declaration of Christ's victory over evil shows an ongoing fear of evil

---

7   Clinton Arnold, *The Colossian Syncretism: The Interface Between Christianity and Folk Belief at Colossae* (Germany: J.C.B. Mohr, 1995), 210.
8   A polytheistic belief that typically focused on devotion of one god because either they were the greatest, or they are the god of their family/tribe/region etc...
9   Arnold, 243.

spirits. How, then, do the points of judgement from the false teachers in verse sixteen relate to the Colossian Philosophy?

First, judgements with regard to food and drink are most likely related to their aestheticism. The teachers believed that since the people were not abstaining extremely enough, the Colossian Christians will be unable to engage in visions and divine experiences. What is interesting is that the Law makes no command to abstain from wine, which further points to the way in which the Philosophy is not an insistence on Torah observance. Moreover, it was believed that evil spirits liked to enter the human body to consume food and drink,[10] and thus abstaining would also have an apotropaic purpose.

Second, the festivals, new moons, and sabbaths of the Philosophy are likely an influence from folk Judaism, redefined by their view of the "elemental spirits." As Joachim Gnilka explains in his commentary, they saw the "times and seasons as an expression of order ruled by cosmic powers who had control over the birth, death, sicknesses, and destiny of humanity."[11] And thus, the observance of these festivals would have included liturgy that called upon angels for protection and deliverance from evil spirits. And like the adaptation of names of gods and goddesses, it is possible that the folk pagan festivals would have been relabeled under the influence of Judaism, such as the celebration of Selene, a moon deity.[12] As Arnold suggests, rather than observing these days in accordance with their Old Testament meanings and their salvation history context, they were adapted by the philosophy result-

---

[10] Ibid., 212.
[11] Joachim Gnilka, *Der Kolosserbrief* (Freiburg: Herder, 1980), 146.
[12] Arnold, 216.

ing in a "discontinuity with the OT meaning and a close connection to the Colossians' fear of hostile forces."[13]

Considering the way these Old Testament rituals were repurposed and redefined to suit and serve the worldview of the Phrygian pagan religions, Paul is telling his audience not to allow these false teachers and adherents of the philosophy to "judge" (*krino*) them as being separate from what the teachers believe is the enlightened, wise, and true way. Nor are they to allow the false teachers to consider them "disqualified" (*katabrabeueto*) from what is rightfully theirs—they can have full assurance of their salvation and union with Christ in his victory over evil because they do not participate in their definition and form of the festivals or observe their strict aestheticism. F.F. Bruce describes something similar in his commentary:

> [T]he Colossians are now told that the observance of these occasions as obligatory is an acknowledgement of the continuing authority of the powers through which such regulations were mediated—the powers that were decisively subjugated by Christ.[14]

If verse 16 was about the Law, did Jesus conquer Moses? Hebrews 3:3-6 would say no; they built the same house. Thus, Paul's primary concern for the Colossian Christians was the risk of them participating in the philosophy's rituals, which include fasting, as well as syncretized festivals and Sabbaths as defined by the philosophy. The risk is that

---

13 Ibid., 215.
14 F. F. Bruce, *The Epistles to the Colossians, to Philemon, and to the Ephesians* (United Kingdom: Eerdmans Publishing Company, 1984), 115.

they would indeed be fearing and submitting to spiritual powers that have been defeated in Christ.

However, as mentioned in a previous chapter, the general nature of Paul's description of the Colossian philosophy means that it *could* be applied to a number of teachings that diminish the person and work of Christ. This may also include a warning against those who promote the observing of what are considered "Jewish Laws and Festivals." But does the letter to the Colossians teach that the ceremonial law, or even the Law as a whole, is abolished? This will be considered when we analyze verse seventeen and fourteen in the following chapter.

CHAPTER 4

DID JESUS END THE LAW?

The advent of Christ was world changing—not only because of the lives he touched during his earthly ministry but also the people and societies that were transformed by the introduction of the Gospel. But more than this, the forgiveness of sins and reconciliation with God means that the way we relate to our Creator has changed. Once we were enemies, now we are his children. There is, however, debate on how we relate to God now that we are in this relationship. From one perspective, the argument goes, "With the coming of Jesus and the 'Christ event,' the Old Testament way of relating to God (i.e., the Law) is done away with and now we follow according to the New Testament only." This position, however, appears in part to be the result of a confusion between "Old Covenant" and "Old Testament,"[1] which is the mixing up of chronology and covenant. Others may argue that most of the Law applies, at least in principle, to varying degrees. But for the vast majority, there is agreement that the ceremonial laws (i.e., festivals, sabbaths, and food laws) are abolished and made irrelevant (either practically or theologically, or both). Among a number of others, there are a couple of passages in Colossians that are commonly used to make both arguments. While evaluating the larger theme of the Christian and the Law would be helpful, the purpose of this chapter (and this book) is to evaluate the use of Colossians in this argument. The assessment of other passages that are used belong to other books.

---

1 Etymologically, they are the same, however Genesis to Malachi is not a covenantal agreement, in particular the Mosaic Covenant. It contains it, but they are not the same thing. See R. L. Watson, *Forgotten Covenant* (Australia: Ark House Press, 2021), 12-13.

Nailed to the Cross

The first passage is verses 13-14, which says:

> And you, who were dead in your trespasses and the uncircumcision of your flesh, God made alive together with him, having forgiven us all our trespasses, by canceling the record of debt that stood against us with its legal demands. This he set aside, nailing it to the cross.
> —Colossians 2:13-14

As outlined in chapter 1, this passage is used to make the claim that it was on the cross that Jesus abolished the Law. Because the crucifixion inaugurated the New Covenant that brings our forgiveness, the Law is no longer binding on the believer. This conclusion is generally the result of reading the term "legal demands" and interpreting it as "the Law." But is this interpretation what the passage is saying?

The context of this verse is that it is a summary of Christ's victory over Satan, sin, and death through his crucifixion and the blessings it gives his people—namely, eternal life, forgiveness of sins, and spiritual protection. Following the argument in verse 14, we see that forgiveness was achieved by the "cancellation of the record of debt." To interpret this passage in the way that has been suggested by some would mean that, in order to forgive us, God abolished the Law that declared us guilty. But with the law gone, how is *anyone* guilty anymore (Rom. 3:19)? What is the standard of sin if God's law is abolished? And therefore, what is the purpose of proclaiming the Gospel? It is worth highlighting that the word Law (*nomos*) is not used in this verse, let alone the chapter, or even the whole letter.[2] When talking about the Law,

---

2 Compare this to the thirty-two times this word appears in Galatians.

Paul uses the term plainly, but in this passage, there are two key terms that are used that help us to understand what it was that was nailed to the cross.

The first is the Greek word *chairographon*. The word literally translates to handwriting, and refers more specifically to a legal note or bond of debt. For example, a papyrus found in Oxyrhynchus[3] states: "the sum total loaned to you by me in accord with the handwritten document (*chairographon*)."[4] This document also most likely contained the conditions and details of the loan, "but perhaps more important, it represented an implicit or explicit personal commitment to repay. This was a 'certificate of indebtedness.'"[5] Thus, being in the context of forgiveness of sin, Paul is using this economic term as a metaphor to describe our indebtedness to God for our sin, and using the imagery of cancelling[6] one's "record of debt" to figuratively describe the forgiveness we have in Christ (cf. Luke 7:42).

The other term is *dogmasin*, which is the word behind the phrase "legal demands." While it can refer to a range of applications, it generally refers to man-made decrees like that from Caesar (Luke 2:1; Acts 17:7), Nebuchadnezzar (Dan. 2:13; 3:10), and the Apostles (Acts 16:4), as well as customs and traditions (Eph. 2:15, Macc. 3:1). But it is never used of God's commands. Nonetheless, it appears to be used in the continuation of Paul's use of a figurative writing. For it "is quite characteristic of Asiatic rhetoric to throw a cornucopia of images and metaphors at the audience, trusting that one or the other will lodge

---

3 Location in Egypt where many ancient papyri have been preserved.
4 In Stephen Geiger, "EXEGETICAL BRIEF: Colossians 2:14 What Was Nailed to the Cross?" *Wisconsin Lutheran Quarterly*, 110, no. 1 (2013), 35.
5 Ibid.
6 *Exaleipsas*: blot out, erase, wipe away.

in their brains."[7] Here, *dogmasin* is being used in two possible ways. One is more narrowly as God's decrees on the punishment and consequences of our sin debt, namely, death (Rom. 6:23), which is an understanding that reflects the relationship of the term to *cheirographon* in conjunction with the historical context of the handwritten note. The other is that *dogmasin* could refer figuratively to the commands of God's Law as a whole which condemns us as sinners. Both could work. In either case, this is not what the text says was blotted out on the cross.

The passage reads that God cancelled *"the record of debt* that stood against us..." And the reason it stood against us was because of the "legal demands"—the Law—that gave the condemnation in the record of debt its power.[8] This can be seen in the example of Christ on the cross when Pilate had the sign "King of the Jews" nailed above Jesus' head. This sign, the *titulus*, "declared...that he was guilty according to the law."[9] But in this case, the charge was against all of Christ's people and God placed it there. Also, as N. T. Wright continues, "As the representative of his people, Jesus dies their death on the cross... This is how God has dealt with sin, so that his people may have new life."[10] Christ deals with sin not by annulling the Law but by satisfying the Law's demands. As Douglas Moo also explains, "What is wiped out is...*the charge of our legal indebtedness*,"[11] and not the commandments

---

7   Ben Witherington, *The Letters to Philemon, the Colossians, and the Ephesians: A Socio-Rhetorical Commentary on the Captivity Epistles* (United Kingdom: Eerdmans Publishing Company, 2007), 154.

8   Robert McL Wilson, *Colossians and Philemon* (United Kingdom: Bloomsbury Academic, 2005), 210.

9   N. T. Wright, *The Epistles of Paul to the Colossians and to Philemon: An Introduction and Commentary* (United Kingdom: Inter-Varsity Press, 1988), 113.

10 Ibid.

11 Douglass Moo, *The Letters to the Colossians and to Philemon* (United Kingdom: Eerdmans Publishing Company, 2008), 209. (Emphasis added.)

themselves. Likewise, in his article on Colossians 2:14, Stephen Geiger explains that it is the *chairographon*, our debt to the Law, that "is nailed to the cross" and therefore it is "in its capacity to condemn…[that] the law has lost its power."[12]

Although Geiger does also argue that our "debt of obedience owed in connection with God's commands" was likewise nailed to the cross,[13] this statement should be understood in the context of meritorious and salvific obedience,[14] rather than general obedience to God. For if because of Christ his disciples no longer have to walk in obedience to God, this would be in contradiction with passages like, "By this we know that we love the children of God, when we love God and obey his commandments" (1 John 5:2) and "What shall we say then? Are we to continue in sin that grace may abound? By no means! How can we who died to sin still live in it" (Rom. 6:1-2, cf. 1 John 3:4). Additionally, it would contradict Paul's instruction to "Walk in Christ" (Col. 2:6, cf. 1:10), a metaphor for godly living and his main point in this chapter.[15] Since merit and salvation were never the purpose of the revealed Law, this is quite possibly speaking to people's consciences who felt obligated to earn favor with God, a thought most likely manipulated by Satan and his demons who wished to distort the Gospel and enslave God's people in guilt (cf. Col. 2:15).

It is also suggested by others that it was the ceremonial aspects of the Law that were nailed to the cross. This is often done by drawing from Ephesians 2, which also uses *dogmasin*. Here, it is argued that the abolishment of "the law of commandments expressed in ordinances

---

12 Geiger, 37.
13 Ibid.
14 Ibid., 34.
15 Barth L. Campbell, "Colossians 2:6-15 as a Thesis: A Rhetorical-Critical Study." *Journal for the Study of Rhetorical Criticism of the New Testament* (2003), 3-4.

[*dogmasin*]" (Eph. 2:15), which ended the "dividing wall of hostility," was the ceremonial law. This is because it is believed that the ceremonial law is what kept the Gentile separate from the Jew. Thus, this theological claim is applied here as well because of the similarity of language and description. As Michael Bird argues, "Adherence to the food laws was a matter of purity and election since they kept the Israelites separate from the other nations and preserved their capacity to worship God in a state of ritual purity."[16] Likewise, as Reynolds explains:

> Christ effectually nailed the ritual law to the cross, so putting an end to the distinctions between Jews and Gentiles and paving the way for the spread of the gospel to all the world through faith in Christ as opposed to coming to God through the sanctuary and its rituals.[17]

Since I have dealt Ephesians 2 in detail elsewhere,[18] and because the focus of this book is on Colossians 2, my response to this claim will be brief. The first issue is that *dogmasin* is used differently in Ephesians 2. There, it refers to the Jewish traditions that were added to the Law to create a man-made ethnic division, whereas here in Colossians 2 it is figuratively applying the conditions of the *chairographon* to the Law. Secondly, the Law as revealed through Moses creates no ethnic barriers. And in the ceremonial aspects in particular, at no point in their descriptions is there an explanation provided that shows it serves to create an ethnic, bloodline, racial boundary. If these observances

---

16 Michael Bird, *Colossians and Philemon: A New Covenant Commentary* (United Kingdom: Lutterworth Press, 2011), 84.

17 Edwin Reynolds, "'Let No One Judge You': Col 2:16-17 in Exegetical Perspective," *Journal of the Adventist Theological Society*, 20/1-2 (2009), 220.

18 See Watson, *Forgotten Covenant*, 297-300.

create any distinction, it is covenant based rather than race based. So, applying this interpretation of Ephesians 2 to Colossians 2 does not work.

Moreover, both the claim made by Bird and Reynolds that the coming of Christ and his atonement for sins opened a new way to approach God is based on faulty assumptions about the ceremonial laws. Firstly, that food laws enabled ritual purity for worship is false. At no point does the Law state that eating unclean food made them unclean. For if it did, then there would be prescribed cleansing rituals in Leviticus in the case of having accidently eaten unclean food, but there are none. Rather, they were to be considered unclean "*by* them" (Lev. 11:8). Secondly, the rituals had a very earthly, temporal focus. Namely, cleansing the flesh so they could draw near the earthly temple. They were never intended as ways to draw near to God in his heavenly temple by cleansing the conscience, as Hebrews makes clear (Heb. 8:4-5; 9:9-14). Rather, as Paul makes clear in Romans, it has *always* been through faith in Christ from the beginning.

So, we can see that this passage does not teach that the Law, neither in part nor the whole, was nailed to the cross; it was our guilt and condemnation that was destroyed by the work of Christ. By dying in our place on the cross, Jesus cancelled and erased the record of debt that condemned us, thus satisfying the *dogmasin*, ending the enemy's[19] power to condemn us. And with this barrier "taken out of the way," we have access to the Lord (cf. Heb. 4:14-16). Thus, Christ's work negates the need and validity to the Colossian Philosophy's claims of fulfilled divine experience.

This reflects and reinforces how verses 13-15 are working in this passage. According to his article on the structure of Colossians 2:6-15,

---

19 Both demonic powers and false teachers who would seek to disqualify us.

Barth Campbell identifies that Colossians 2:13-15 is an "authoritative citation" that supports the truth of our union with Christ and the certainty we can have in the person and work of Christ (Col. 2:7). Moreover, contrary to the Colossian Philosophy, we can also find our fullness and the full experience of God in Him alone.[20] In his discussion on verse thirteen, Campbell explains how the "forgiveness of our transgressions" is connected to our "being made alive" in Christ.[21] Thus, the reference to *cheirographon* in verse 14 functions as a legal metaphor of "an accusatory record of violations of the Mosaic law (*tois dogmasin*). The statement of indebtedness that testified against us was erased. God nailed it to the cross...Christ's death sufficed as a payment for our sins."[22] Thus, knowing the certainty of their forgiveness, there is no need for Paul's readers to pursue the false teachers' "empty and vain philosophy."

Therefore, it was not the Law that was nailed to the cross. Rather, it was our debt that was "put to death," and to claim that this verse teaches we are no longer obligated to obey the Law in any way is exegetically unfounded.

The Shadow of Things to Come

As mentioned in chapter 1, the other passage used to claim that the Law is done away with is verse 17. Having just instructed the Colossians not to allow anyone to pass judgment on them regarding food, drink, festivals and Sabbaths in verse 16, Paul explains that "These are a shadow of the things to come, but the substance belongs to Christ." Thus, from this verse, it is argued that the Law (or at least

---

20 Campbell, 5-6.
21 Ibid., 13.
22 Ibid.

the "ceremonial law" since they are the elements in focus) is no longer relevant because Christ has now fulfilled their purpose—namely, as a foreshadowing of Christ. To further support this argument, the following illustration is used in one variation or another:

> Imagine that your spouse has been gone for a very long time and all you have had is a picture to help you think of him/her. You go to the airport and he/she gets off the plane. You go running towards him/her, but when you get there you fall on the ground and start kissing his/her shadow and trying to hug the shadow. You start saying, "Oh I love you shadow, I love you so much shadow!" He/she would probably look at you like you were nuts. He/She would probably say, "Hey! I'm right here! Love me, not my shadow!"[23]

The story does make a couple of valid points. Encountering and connecting with Jesus is certainly superior to the festivals and sabbaths that point to him, and we must therefore keep Christ, and not our "ceremonies," central in our lives. Also, the argument that Jesus' person and ministry was foreshadowed by the ceremonial law is certainly true. As Gregory Beale explains, "Jesus 'fulfilled' the 'law' and 'the prophets' by fulfilling in his actions and words the OT's direct verbal prophecies foreshadowing events (e.g. the Passover lamb) and institutions (e.g. sacrifices and temple)..."[24] The book of Hebrews also makes use of the "shadow" and "substance" language when talking about the sacrifices

---

23 Chris Lee, "A Study of the Covenants: Chapter 11," *Life Insurance Ministries*, https://www.lifeassuranceministries.org/studies/covenants/covenants11.html.

24 G. K. Beale, "Colossians," *Commentary on the New Testament Use of the Old Testament* (United Kingdom: Baker Publishing Group, 2007), 862.

at the Temple to highlight the supremacy and sufficiency of the atonement and ministry of Christ (Heb. 8:4-6; 10:1-18). Nonetheless, does this passage in Colossians 2:17 teach that now that Jesus, the superior substance, has come, the law has no relevance to the believer?

The first issue is with identifying the whole phrase in verse 16 as the ceremonial law. Not only is the division of the Torah into the three distinct categories of moral, civil, and ceremonial difficult, arbitrary, and extrabiblical, but as mentioned in the previous chapter, these were practices adapted and promoted by the Colossian Philosophers for apotropaic and aesthetic purposes. Moreover, there are no drink restrictions in the Law. However, as Reynolds argues:

> [T]he feasts, new moons, and sabbaths were the times when these various offerings were to be made. It is interesting also that grain (food) and drink offerings were included along with burnt offerings, sin offerings, and peace offerings.[25]

That being the case, food and drink are most likely being used as a shorthand for rituals and sacrifices, rather than kosher laws—which is quite reasonable since the idea of food laws being a foreshadow of Christ is difficult to explain and not a connection that the New Testament makes.[26] In the context of the Colossian Philosophy, however, it is more likely that they are connected to their aesthetic practices as well as their cultic rituals. Hence, Paul is saying not to allow anyone to disqualify you because you do not participate in these traditions.

---

25 Reynolds, 213-215 (cf. Neh 10:32-33, Hos 2:11, 1Chr 23:30-31, 2Chr 2:4, 8:12-13, 31:3, Isa 1:13-14).

26 While it might be argued that Jesus satisfies the ceremonial purification they provide, as mentioned above, the food laws never provided this function.

Nonetheless, as described previously, the general nature of the passage means that it could possibly be applied to the original Old Testament context that was adapted by the false teachers. Indeed, no one can disqualify a disciple of Christ as being a true Christian and genuinely redeemed on these grounds, whether by their observance or abstaining from them, because they are not the foundation of our salvation. Faith is. Thus, on the one hand this passage does teach in a general sense that the ceremonial aspects of the Law, whether in their original context or adapted by pagan mystics, do not grant us favor with Christ. But that in itself does not mean that they are irrelevant. We are not saved by baptism, a shadow of our union with Christ, either. Does that make the practice irrelevant? Paul is adamant in many of his letters that we are not saved by good works, but he is also adamant that we need to live out our salvation by living in obedience to God's commands. What, therefore, is verse 17 teaching?

First, we need to note the tense of the arrival of "the things." The passage does not read "These are a shadow of the things *which have come*," but rather "a shadow of things *to come*." The word for coming (*mellonton*) refers to things that are to happen in the future. For example, in Revelation the angels cry out "Woe, woe, woe to those who dwell on the earth, at the blasts of the other trumpets that the three angels are about to (*mellonton*) blow" (Rev. 8:13)! It is also typically used of events that are destined by divine authority to happen. For example, "This was to fulfill the word that Jesus had spoken to show by what kind of death he was going to (*emellen*) die" (John 18:32). Although this is talking about the past, this is because the participle *mellonton* takes on the tense of the main verb, spoken, which is past tense. Nonetheless, when Jesus said it, it was future tense. In the case of Colossians 2:17, the main verb is "to be" (*estin*), which is present tense, meaning the things that the shadows point to are still on their way.

As Robert Wilson explains, "the participle is used absolutely with the meaning 'future, to come'...."[27] Similarly, Troy Martin remarks:

> The tense is present and affirms that these things are now shadows. These commentators translate the past tense and conclude that these stipulations have ended.... In spite of this eisegesis, the text affirms a present, albeit temporary, validity to the shadow.[28]

Thus, the festivals and sabbaths and sacrifices must point to a more complete fulfillment in the future. Indeed, Christ's death on the cross and resurrection were the beginning, but the fullness has not yet arrived. The Passover still awaits our complete deliverance from sin, evil, and death. First Fruits awaits the complete harvest of all the nations. Pentecost awaits our complete sanctification and glorification in the New Heavens and Earth (Rom. 8:30; 1 Cor. 15:40-44, 53). The Day of Trumpets awaits the return of Christ our victorious King. The Day of Atonement awaits the final judgment of the wicked and salvation of Christ's sheep. The Feast of Tabernacles awaits our uninhibited dwelling with God (Rev. 21:3). And the Sabbath awaits our final eternal rest from the hardships of this world as well as God's full and perfect reign. In this case, therefore, in the analogy of the plane trip and the kissing of the shadow, based on the grammar of this verse and the eschatological meaning of the festivals and sabbaths, the plane has not landed yet. They're on the way, so we still have the shadow of the plane on the tarmac. They are a shadow of "things to come."

---

27 Wilson, 220.
28 Troy Martin, "But Let Everyone Discern the Body of Christ (Colossians 2:17)," *Journal of Biblical Literature* 114, no. 2 (1995), 249 fn 1.

Second, even if it could be shown that the true and complete fulfillment has arrived, why would that mean their discontinuance? Consider the practice of Passover and the Lord's Supper. Both were instituted as "shadows" the night before the events they reflected, namely the Exodus and Crucifixion. Their symbology pointed to the theological realities contained in these significant moments in salvation history. The event came and went (meaning the "substance" arrived), and yet God's people were to continue practicing them. Imagine an Israelite in the time of David saying, "Why are we doing Passover? It was a shadow pointing to our deliverance from Egypt. The substance has come! Why are we holding onto the lesser form?" And no one would argue, "Let's discontinue communion because that was just a shadow of the death of Jesus; the substance that has arrived." So even though the more complete meaning of the festivals and sabbaths has arrived, wouldn't that just mean that, like communion, such observances are a moment to look back? And since there is a more complete meaning to be fulfilled, they are also moments to look forward (1 Cor. 11:26)? All that has changed is the chronological relationship we share with what they point to.

Third, it appears that Paul is countering the Colossian Philosophy, which has adapted these practices, not the original practices themselves. He is reminding his audience that the sacrifices and festivals have their meaning in the person and mission of Christ, and do not exist to punish the flesh, gain access to God, and fight off evil. Troy Martin in his article on Colossians 2:16-17 suggests that the Greek grammar of these verses means that the food and festivals are not functioning here as shadows that have been replaced with Christ.[29] This is primarily due to the use of the "adversative conjunction" *de*, which can only join two clauses of the same type,[30] meaning "these are a Shadow of things to come" (relative clause) and "the substance belongs to Christ" (independent clause) cannot be connected.[31] Martin explains that to treat the relative clause as independent, which has been done traditionally, "contradicts the grammatical construction of the text."[32] The other independent clause is in verse 16: "don't let anyone judge you…" Thus, *these* two clauses are connected. In which case, "The negative member is stated first; the contrasting positive member introduced by an adversative conjunction occurs second."[33] He also explains that because of the two parallel clauses that use an ellipsis (*estin* [are]), "Only a few of the elements of the first clause are repeated in the second clause and the remaining parallel elements must be supplied."[34] Therefore, based on the grammatical details and construction of verses sixteen and seventeen, Martin offers the following translation:

> Therefore do not let anyone critique you by [*your or her/his?*][35] eating and drinking or by [*your or her/his?*] participation in a feast, a new moon, or sabbaths, which things are a shadow of future realities, but let everyone discern the body of Christ

---

29 They do indeed foreshadow the person and work of Christ, but it is not Paul's purpose here to describe them in a manner akin to Plato's cave analogy of shadow and true form. See Martin, 250-255.
30 Ibid., 250.
31 Ibid., 251.
32 Ibid.
33 Ibid., 252.
34 Ibid., 254.
35 Since the text is unclear whether the judgement is based on the Colossian Christians' or the False Teachers' observance or abstaining.

> by [*your or her/his?*] *eating and drinking or by* [*your or her/his?*] *participation in a feast, a new moon, or sabbaths, which things are a shadow of future realities.*[36]

This translation reflects the way Paul is reminding his audience of the way these festivals and sacrifices reveal the person and work of Christ, and that the Colossians are to "discern" them as positive because of this revelatory truth within them. Indeed, it appears that the passage is saying that one is to discern who belongs to the body, which is the antithesis of "judging," by this understanding. The false teachers remove Jesus and the true biblical meaning from these practices. Instead of their observance being an expression of their worship of God because of his mighty deeds, they repurpose these practices for superstitious, self-seeking, and apotropaic purposes in the veneration of false gods. The true members of the body, on the other hand, recognize the true meaning of these practices. It is also likely that, since Paul is explaining that these practices are shadows of future realities, the ones practicing them and receiving judgement are the Colossians. As Martin suggests, "exegetes should seriously consider the possibility that Christian practices, and not those of the opponents, are criticized in Col 2:16, 18."[37] This makes sense in light of the aesthetic and mystical elements of the philosophy, which would cause them to tell the Colossian Christians that they should be abstaining, or even that their approach and understanding means that they're not doing it properly. Therefore, it is possible that Paul could very well be telling the Christians in Colossae, "Don't let anyone judge you for the way you

---

36   Martin, 254.
37   Ibid., 255.

celebrate with food and drink,[38] or for how you observe festivals and sabbaths, because in doing so, you are honoring Christ for his works and anticipating their fulfilment in the last day."

Therefore, considering the context and purpose of this instruction in Paul's letter as an application of the certainty his readers have in their union with Christ, we can see that the grammatical details of the words and phrases with regards to their tense and construction of meaning show how Paul is reminding the Christians of the true nature of the festivals and rituals as opposed to the Colossian Philosophy's distorted definition. Paul is not saying that these aspects of the Law are now irrelevant and discontinued. Rather, his purpose is to rescue their meaning from pagan syncretism and protect the Christians from an erroneous philosophy.

---

38 A potential reference to 1 Cor. 11:29.

CHAPTER 5
CONCLUSION

The content and theology of the letter to the Colossians is valuable, especially in this modern day when syncretism and relative truth is popular in the world around us. Indeed, there are a growing number of Christians who are wanting to experience more of God, which is certainly in line with Scripture: "One thing have I asked of the Lord, that will I seek after: that I may dwell in the house of the Lord all the days of my life, to gaze upon the beauty of the Lord and to inquire in his temple" (Psalm 27:4). However, many of these Christians are flirting with New Age practices to do so. The letter to the Colossians speaks to this issue in the way that it counteracts the worldly wisdom of "human tradition" and "empty deceit" by exalting Christ and revealing to us his supremacy and sufficiency. As George Ladd explains when commenting on the themes of Paul's writing, "the wisdom of this world can never commend a person to God, for it is foolishness... The principles of the world, which include human speculations and traditions and even religion, are antithetical to Christ (Col. 2:8)."[1] And because of its general description of the false teacher's philosophy, it speaks to any worldview that sets itself up in opposition to the truth of Christ.

This general nature, however, is what makes interpretation of the specifics of the letter difficult—in particular, the nature of the heresy Paul was rebuking. In order to make application from any Scripture, knowing what is being corrected is important. However, as mentioned in the introduction, there are clues that help us. As we have seen in the pages of this book, Paul was not rebuking Judaizers who were insisting

---

1   George Ladd, *A Theology of the New Testament* (United States: Eerdmans, 1993), 438.

Conclusion

that the Colossian Christians follow "Jewish customs." And neither was he trying to teach us that the Law, or even just the ceremonial law, was abolished and irrelevant. Rather, based on historical and archaeological evidence of the area that shows it as a region known for syncretistic religion, a folk pagan religion with mystery cult elements that had adapted elements of Judaism from the Jewish population was now incorporating Christian elements and appealing to the church in Colossae. As part of their appropriation, they had redefined the festivals, sabbaths, and rituals mentioned in the Law, and perhaps even the Lord's supper too. These false teachers were telling the Colossian Christians that they had the superior way to connect with God, namely through their folk paganistic practices and traditions such as visions and spiritual experiences. Thus, they were judging and disqualifying the Christians as either inferior, or "not real Christians." It was against this worldly philosophy that Paul was speaking, not against expressions of the "ceremonial law." And when Paul spoke of "canceling the record of debt that stood against us with its legal demands" and having it "nailed to the cross," this was a metaphorical image of our forgiveness, not a declaration that the Law was annulled to bring our forgiveness. A close reading shows that it was in fact the "record of debt" that was destroyed. If God could forgive us by deleting the Law, Christ died for nothing.

Granted, as mentioned in an earlier chapter, Paul's warning in verse 16 to "let no one pass judgment on you in questions of food and drink, or with regard to a festival or a new moon or a Sabbath" could be legitimately applied to those who condemn other Christians for either observing or not observing them. One cannot judge a follower of Christ's status based on whether they observe them, and that could be a valid application of Paul's argument. Nonetheless, that is not the issue here. The debate regarding the Law is whether the ceremonial aspects are relevant; Paul's argument in Colossians 2 is that how one practices these things does not define their relationship with Christ. These are two *different topics*. Thus, in order to argue that the ceremonial aspects of the Law, or even the Law as a whole, are done away with, one would need to look to other passages to make that claim.

ABOUT THE AUTHOR
WHO IS R. L. WATSON?

Ryan Watson is an author and Bible teacher with both Undergraduate and Postgraduate qualifications in Theology. He is committed to equipping Christians in building a theology with an all-of-scripture approach to interpreting God's Word. Additionally, Watson is passionate about helping followers of Christ understand the Bible's historical and linguistic context and assisting Bible readers in recognizing God's goodness, sovereignty, and glory, and the beauty of His Gospel.

Ryan's books include *Forgotten Covenant* (2021) and *Why then the Law?* (2020).

Ryan lives in Brisbane, Australia, with his wife and four boys. He currently works as a High School English teacher. Connect with Ryan at his website: rlwatsonauthor.com

BIBLIOGRAPHY

Arnold, C. *The Colossian Syncretism: The Interface Between Christianity and Folk Belief at Colossae.* Germany: J.C.B. Mohr (Paul Siebeck), 1995.

Bargerhuff, Eric J. *The Most Misused Verses in the Bible: Surprising Ways God's Word Is Misunderstood.* Grand Rapids, MI: Baker Publishing Group, 2012.

Beale, G. K. *Colossians and Philemon.* Grand Rapids, MI: Baker Publishing Group, 2019.

_____ "Colossians." *Commentary on the New Testament Use of the Old Testament.* United Kingdom: Baker Publishing Group, 2007.

Bird, M. *Colossians and Philemon: A New Covenant Commentary.* United Kingdom: Lutterworth Press, 2011.

Bruce, F. *The Epistles to the Colossians, to Philemon, and to the Ephesians.* United Kingdom: Eerdmans Publishing Company, 1984.

Burkert, W. *Ancient Mystery Cults.* United Kingdom: Harvard University Press, 1987.

Campbell, B. "Colossians 2:6-15 as a Thesis: A Rhetorical-Critical Study." *Journal for the Study of Rhetorical Criticism of the New Testament.* 2003: 1-15. https://rhetjournal.net/RhetJournal/Articles_files/Campbell.pdf

Garland, D. *Colossians, Philemon.* Grand Rapids, MI: Zondervan, 2009.

Geiger, S. "EXEGETICAL BRIEF: Colossians 2:14 What Was Nailed to the Cross?" *Wisconsin Lutheran Quarterly*, 110, no. 1, 2013: 34-40. http://essays.wisluthsem.org:8080/handle/123456789/1794

Gnilka, J. *Der Kolosserbrief.* Freiburg: Herder, 1980.

Holland, Brian. "The Book of Colossians: Colossians 2:9-15." *Ignite City Church.* June 26, 2022. https://youtu.be/pXALiCDARQ8.

Ladd, G. *A Theology of the New Testament.* United States: Eerdmans, 1993.

Lee, C. "A Study of the Covenants: Chapter 11." *lifeassuranceministries.org.* https://www.lifeassuranceministries.org/studies/covenants/covenants11.html

Martin, T. "But Let Everyone Discern the Body of Christ (Colossians 2:17)." *Journal of Biblical Literature* 114, no. 2, 1995: 249–55. https://doi.org/10.2307/3266938.

Miller, John. "Complete In Christ - Part 2." *Revival Christian Fellowship.* July 2, 2017. https://www.revival.tv/sermons/colossians/complete-in-christ-part-2/.

Moo, D. *The Letters to the Colossians and to Philemon.* United Kingdom: Eerdmans Publishing Company, 2008.

Phillips, R. *Hebrews.* New Jersey: P & R Publishing, 2006.

Reynolds, E. "'Let No One Judge You': Col 2:16-17 in Exegetical Perspective." *Journal of the Adventist Theological Society,* 20/1-2 (2009): 208-222.

Vaughn, C. "Colossians." *The Expositors Bible Commentary* - Vol 11. Grand Rapids, MI: Zondervan, 1978.

Watson, R. *Forgotten Covenant.* Australia: Ark House Press, 2021.

Wilson, R. *Colossians and Philemon.* United Kingdom: Bloomsbury Academic, 2005.

Witherington, B. *The Letters to Philemon, the Colossians, and the Ephesians: A Socio-Rhetorical Commentary on the Captivity Epistles.* United Kingdom: Eerdmans Publishing Company, 2007.

BIBLIOGRAPHY

Wright, N.T. *The Epistles of Paul to the Colossians and to Philemon: An Introduction and Commentary.* United Kingdom: Inter-Varsity Press, 1988.

www.ingramcontent.com/pod-product-compliance
Lightning Source LLC
Chambersburg PA
CBHW060354050426
42449CB00011B/2982